Fact Finders®

The Story of Sanitation

STINKING SEWERS!

WHAT HAPPENS TO OUR WASTE?

by Riley Flynn

raintree

a Capstone company — publishers for children

Raintree is an imprint of Capstone Global Library Limited, a company incorporated in England and Wales having its registered office at 264 Banbury Road, Oxford, OX2 7DY – Registered company number: 6695582

www.raintree.co.uk
myorders@raintree.co.uk

Edited by Anna Butzer
Designed by Bobbie Nuytten
Original illustrations © Capstone Global Library Limited 2019
Picture research by Morgan Walters
Production by Kris Wilfahrt
Originated by Capstone Global Library Ltd
Printed and bound in India

ISBN 978 1 4747 6425 4
22 21 20 19 18
10 9 8 7 6 5 4 3 2 1

British Library Cataloguing in Publication Data
A full catalogue record for this book is available from the British Library.

Acknowledgements
We would like to thank the following for permission to reproduce photographs: Alamy: ART Collection, 10, top 28; Getty Images: sola deo gloria, 9; iStockphoto: BlackJack3D, 27; Shutterstock: Abel Feyman, 8, Aleks Melnik, Cover, Alon Othnay, Cover, AuntSpray, 15, Avatar_023, 17, Dimitar Sotirov, Cover, djmilic, 1, focal point, 26, I WALL, (paper) design element throughout, karamysh, 5, Kekyalyaynen, 20, Lyudvig Aristarhovich, 19, Mei Yi, bottom left 14, bottom middle 14, bottom right 14, michaelheim, 23, 29, Milosz_G, 13, Nomad_Soul, 11, Rawpixel.com, 25, Renata Sedmakova, 22, saknakorn, 4, bottom 28, stockphoto-graf, 24, tele52, 18, Thuwanan Krueabudda, 21, Toa55, 16, Vladimir Mulder, 6, Wanna Thongpao, 7, Zurijeta, 12

Every effort has been made to contact copyright holders of material reproduced in this book. Any omissions will be rectified in subsequent printings if notice is given to the publisher.

love your
library

Buckinghamshire Libraries

Search, renew or reserve online 24/7

www.buckscc.gov.uk/libraries

24 hour renewal line
0303 123 0035

Enquiries
01296 382415

@Bucks_Libraries

CONTENTS

CHAPTER 1

CHAPTER 2

CHAPTER 3

CHAPTER 4

CHAPTER 1
A SEWER RUNS THROUGH IT

The toilet, commode, porcelain throne, bog or loo. No matter what you call it, it's the place to go when you need relief. Everybody does their business – numbers one and two – but not everyone knows what happens after they flush. Most of us don't think twice about what goes down the toilet . . . as long as it doesn't come back up.

Toilets use different amounts of water to flush. Some older versions can use up to 26 litres (7 gallons) per flush!

4

Flushable toilets help keep our homes and towns clean. Sinks are great for washing hands and dishes. Showers give us privacy when it is time to rinse off. But have you ever wondered what happens after the water we use goes down the drain? Have you ever wondered where all that stuff goes? No? Well it's time to find out!

Help conserve water by having showers instead of baths. Keep your shower short to save more water.

What is waste water?

Did you know that anything that goes down a drain is classified as sewage? Another term for sewage is waste water. Waste water is any water that has been used by humans. Waste water often contains faeces (poo), urine (wee) and cleaning chemicals. In the UK, the average person produces nearly 150 litres (40 gallons) of waste water per day. That's a lot of dirty water! That's why sewers and waste water treatment centres are so important.

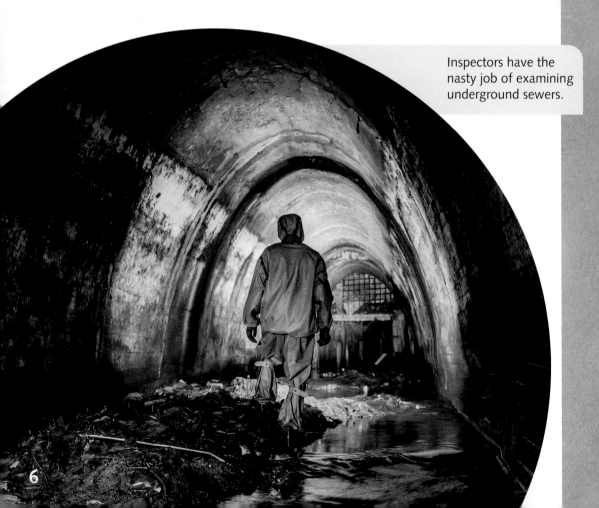

Inspectors have the nasty job of examining underground sewers.

Treatment plants reduce **pollutants** in waste water to a level nature can handle.

We live on a planet that is 70 per cent water. But only a small percentage of it is available for humans to use. There is not enough water on the planet for all the people living here. That's why it's important that waste water goes through a recycling process at treatment facilities. Sewers are a huge part of the process that waste water has to go through.

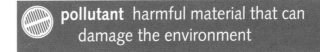

pollutant harmful material that can damage the environment

CHAPTER 2

PLUMBING THROUGH THE AGES

Imagine what your town would be like if sewer systems didn't exist. Waste water would flow through the streets, and an awful smell would constantly fill the air. Every now and then, it would rain, and the waste and its smelly odour would be washed away. But wait! That waste, *human* waste, would just be washed into nearby rivers or lakes. Before sewer systems were created in the late 1800s, that's how people used to live.

Ancient plumbing

The Indus people lived 4,000 years ago in what is now Pakistan. They had a system of street drains and indoor toilets. The Indus poured water down the drains which pushed waste into a system of brick pipes. The Indus wisely directed these pipes away from their sources of drinking water. This system stopped people getting ill.

FACT An early sewer system in the palace of Minos at Knossos in ancient Greece used **terracotta** pipes.

The Romans built an early version of public toilets.

Pots and pits

Unfortunately, later civilizations didn't continue using the plumbing methods created by the Indus people. Instead of toilets, people used **chamber pots**. Towns and cities didn't have pipes to take waste away, so people sometimes had **cesspools** in their basements or back gardens. A cesspool is a hole where human waste, rotting food and other rubbish are thrown.

Some people emptied their chamber pots into the streets or into rivers or lakes.

 terracotta fired clay that is cheap to use and lasts a long time

chamber pot bowl that people used as a toilet

cesspool pit in the ground that holds human waste and other rubbish

Filthy cities and first flushes

Queen Elizabeth I's godson, John Harington invented the first water closet in the 1590s. It was an early version of the flushable toilet we know and love today. More than 200 years passed before Harington's idea caught on because most people saw no reason to install toilets. To them, it was easier to dump the contents of a chamber pot out of the window. At that time, there were no sewer systems so there was nowhere for the waste to go. Without sewers, waste ended up outside, one way or another.

John Harington
(1561–1612)

But as the population grew in Europe and the United States, so did the number of cesspools. The smell of human waste hung in the air. And the germs from the waste eventually polluted the drinking water. Terrible diseases killed thousands of people. It was time to do something to keep waste off the streets and keep the waterways clean. People needed sewers. By the late 1800s, many large cities had them.

SAVED BY SEWERS

In the 1500s many Europeans developed a fear of bathing. They believed that if they got wet they would become ill. No one knew that it was really the germs and bacteria in the water that was making them sick. Today we know that illnesses can be spread through human waste and dirty water. This makes us even more grateful for our sewer systems.

CHAPTER 3

FROM FLUSH TO FINISH

Think about all the times you've flushed the toilet, done the washing up, brushed your teeth or had a shower. Where does all that used water go? Waste water doesn't just disappear after it goes down the drain. Today many people's toilets, sinks, showers and other water fixtures in their homes are all connected.

Scrape any leftover food into the bin before washing up. Food scraps can clog up pipes fast and cause a big problem.

Depending on the type of house or flat you live in, you may be able to see your soil pipe. The soil pipe is connected to your toilet. It carries waste water away from your home and to the sewers.

The waste water flows downwards from small underground pipes to bigger underground pipes. Each pipe goes deeper and deeper into the ground.

Some waste water pipes can be easily seen. Others are hidden behind walls.

13

Journey through the pipes

Eventually all pipes connect to the main sewer. This is a large pipe deep underground. Some main sewers are large enough for an adult to stand up in. Even bigger main sewers have a wide stream in the middle and walkways on each side. The water flowing in the main sewer holds all the waste water from every sink, toilet and bath in the area. That gunky water makes its way to a sewage treatment plant.

UNDERGROUND ACCESS

Manhole covers are an important part of the sewer system. These metal plates provide access to the pipes underneath our towns and cities. Thanks to manholes, maintenance workers can easily climb down into the sewers to fix any problems. Some countries decorate their manhole covers with designs. Pretty and practical!

WASTE WATER SYSTEM

manhole

after the flush

to sewage treatment plant

direction of waste water flow

What happens at the sewage treatment plant?

What happens to that gigantic underground stream of water, bodily waste and other nasty stuff? Before the late 1800s, that waste water was dumped directly back into rivers. Eventually people realized that dirty water was making them unwell and that waste water needed to be cleaned. Today waste water is cleaned at treatment plants.

FACT More than 11 billion litres of waste water is collected by sewers in the UK each day and taken to one of 9,000 sewage treatment plants.

Waste water treatment plants help keep dirty water like this out of our lakes and rivers.

At the treatment plant

At treatment plants, waste water goes through several stages: screening, primary treatment, secondary treatment and tertiary treatment, which can include a **disinfection** process. Before waste water can be treated, the solid objects that found their way into the sewer need to be removed. During the screening process, special screens trap large pieces of rubbish such as sticks, leaves, wet-wipes and more. This rubbish is dried and taken away to landfills or incinerated.

Sewage treatment plant workers make sure that the waste water is being properly cleaned.

disinfect use chemicals to kill germs

Primary treatment

After the solids are strained from the waste water, it is still filled with human waste, poisonous gases and germs. These things could pollute rivers and harm people and animals. The waste water is moved to **sedimentation** tanks. Any solids still in the waste water sink to the bottom of the tanks. These solids are called sludge. The sludge is pumped away for further treatment, and the waste water is moved to large tanks for secondary treatment.

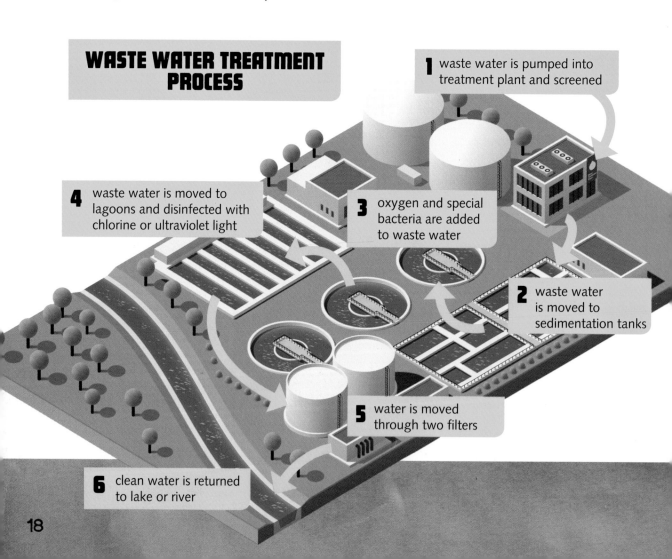

WASTE WATER TREATMENT PROCESS

1 waste water is pumped into treatment plant and screened

2 waste water is moved to sedimentation tanks

3 oxygen and special bacteria are added to waste water

4 waste water is moved to lagoons and disinfected with chlorine or ultraviolet light

5 water is moved through two filters

6 clean water is returned to lake or river

Secondary treatment

Waste water is moved to large tanks where workers add oxygen and special bacteria to it. This is called secondary treatment. Oxygen makes the bacteria grow quickly. As the bacteria grow, they eat the pollutants in the water. When the bacteria run out of food, they die. The water left behind is a lot cleaner than it was before, but the waste water still passes through two more **filters**. One uses sand, and the other uses charcoal. These filters help remove any remaining germs.

FACT Primary and secondary treatments remove about 85 to 95 per cent of pollutants before the treated waste water is disinfected.

sedimentation process that cleans water by allowing small particles to sink to the bottom and be removed

filter device that cleans liquids or gases as they pass through it

Look at the bubbles on top of the waste water in the tank. That is what happens when oxygen is added to it.

Disinfection

Finally, the waste water begins a process called **lagooning**, where it is pumped into large ponds. Any remaining solid waste settles to the bottom, leaving clean water on the top. In some places, plants are grown in the lagoons because plants eat even more harmful bacteria.

a waste water treatment plant

lagooning process during which waste water sits in artificial ponds, allowing solid waste to sink to the bottom

As the waste water is pumped into these ponds, it is disinfected. Some treatment plants use chlorine, the same chemical that cleans swimming pools. Many animals drink treated water once it is released back into lakes and rivers. Unfortunately, studies have shown that chlorine causes cancer in some animals. Because of this, many treatment plants now use ultraviolet light to disinfect water instead.

Water is exposed to ultraviolet light in a water treatment pond.

Sludge treatment

After the sludge and waste water have been separated, the sludge is moved from storage tanks to a **dewatering** centre. There, sludge is moved to a large, rotating machine called a centrifuge. The centrifuge acts in a similar way to the spin cycle of a washing machine. The **centrifugal force** from spinning fast separates the rest of the water from the sludge.

dewatering removal of water from solid material

centrifugal force physical force that causes a body rotating around a centre to move away from the centre

Some treatment plants don't have dewatering machines. At those plants the sludge is moved through a pipeline, or by a sludge boat, to a plant with a dewatering machine.

Some treated waste water can be used to make energy. It can also be recycled to make water that can be used on farms. Some countries, including Australia and Singapore, make recycled drinking water out of treated sewage.

CHAPTER 4

HOW OUR WASTE WATER AFFECTS OUR WORLD

Waste water needs to be properly treated before it can be disposed of. If it's not, it can **contaminate** water and harm plants and animals in rivers or oceans.

contaminate make dirty or unfit for use

Sewage that has been properly treated can still cause problems. Researchers have found that microscopic plastic fibres can make it through the waste water treatment plants. These particles have been found in fish and shellfish that humans eat. They have also been found in our tap water. Researchers believe these small plastic fibres come from washing clothes made from synthetic fabrics.

Buying clothing with natural fibres instead of synthetic can help reduce the amount of plastic in our water.

Make a difference

The way we treat sewage now is a lot better than in the past. But billions of litres of partially treated sewage still make it into our lakes and rivers every year. Even sewage that hasn't been treated can sometimes get into our water sources. This can be caused by sewer overflows or leaking pipes.

With the shortage of clean water, it is important that we do all we can to help keep water safe. It is everyone's responsibility to make sure household products are properly thrown away.

Sewers make our world a much cleaner place to live, and it is our job to help keep them working properly.

FACT Cleaning products with hazardous chemicals should never be poured down a drain. These toxins could end up polluting a river, lake or stream.

TIMELINE

500 BC
Underground sewers were built in ancient Rome.

1590s
John Harington designed the first flushing toilet and installed one for his godmother, Queen Elizabeth I. It released waste into a cesspool.

1866
Most of London is connected to a sewer network designed by Joseph Bazalgette.

1388
England outlaws dumping of waste in streets and public waterways.

1851
The flush toilet is first introduced to the public.

500 BC   1400   1800

1981

The International Drinking Water Supply and Sanitation Decade is launched by the UN to support clean water and sanitation worldwide.

1883

The first septic tank is introduced in the United States.

1923

The world's first large-scale sludge plant is built in Wisconsin, USA.

1985

The Great Pacific Garbage Patch is discovered in the Pacific Ocean. Large amounts of plastic, chemical sludge and other debris are pushed together by ocean movement.

1900

1990

GLOSSARY

centrifugal force physical force that causes a body rotating around a centre to move away from the centre

cesspool pit in the ground that holds human waste and other rubbish

chamber pot bowl that people used as a toilet

contaminate make dirty or unfit for use

dewatering removal of water from solid material

disinfect use chemicals to kill germs

filter device that cleans liquids or gases as they pass through it; water can be cleaned by going through a filter made of sand, gravel or charcoal

lagooning process during which waste water sits in artificial ponds, allowing solid waste to sink to the bottom

pollutant harmful material that can damage the environment

sedimentation process that cleans water by allowing small particles to sink to the bottom and be removed

terracotta fired clay that is cheap to use and lasts a long time

FIND OUT MORE

BOOKS

Environment Infographics (Infographics), Chris Oxlade
(Raintree, 2014)

How Things Work (See Inside), Conrad Mason (Usborne, 2009)

The Story Behind Toilets (True Stories), Elizabeth Raum
(Raintree, 2010)

The Water Cycle (Earth by Numbers), Nancy Dickmann
(Raintree, 2018)

WEBSITES

Learn more about what happens to our sewage at:
www.bbc.com/bitesize/clips/z7jkjxs

Find out more about the first flushing toilets at:
www.dkfindout.com/uk/science/amazing-inventions/flushing-toilet

COMPREHENSION QUESTIONS

1. What would our world be like without waste water treatment plants? How would life be different?

2. What are some ways you can help keep our sewers working properly and keep our water sources clean?

3. How much waste water does an average person in the UK produce in a day? What are some ways we can cut back on water usage?

INDEX